STANDING

Shane Johnson

BookLeaf Publishing

India | USA | UK

Presentation by *BookLeaf Publishing*

Web: www.bookleafpub.com

E-mail: info@bookleafpub.com

ISBN: 9789358739282

First edition 2021

FOREWORD

I wrote this book during a time of self-imposed reflection and willful growth. As a queer black man, my identity has always been my prison, and it wasn't until recently that I learned it would grow to be my greatest gift. Who I am, who I was born to be, the version of myself I choose to create and build upon is my sole inheritance. In a world where all who came before me could leave nothing but their blood and bones, this was the first step in my journey. Realizing that all that pain could be turned into prosperity, if only I allowed it.

This book is the first of many accounts of what it is to always choose love — love for oneself, for others, for what may come, for what has come. This is a guiding light for everyone who struggles to believe that they are worthy or capable of love. If you fear the sound of compassion has been drowned out by the endless clangor of hate, disdain, or detestation. I challenge you to pluck the string once more and hear how heartedly that chord strikes, if only you let it.

To all who schemed, plotted, and willed my demise: I am standing, still.

I dedicate this page to my loving siblings, Danayah and Tykhil. The two of you have fought unendingly to create a space where I could exist freely. Where I could find righteousness in the love I offer, and security in the love I receive. You two have each been two steps ahead, behind, and beside me protecting me from anything that would wish harm on me. If I haven't said it enough, I love you. Thank you for giving me the opportunity to do so.

To my wonderful mother, who knows war so well she taught her son to protect himself before daylight ever reached our threshold. Who taught me that for people like us, sometimes the dark would always be a better home. This is an ode to our fight, our battle for all that we believe in. This is a testimony to our love, a record of how the strongest woman this planet will know birthed the strongest of children. An attestation to all we did, do, and will do to change the world.

1 OF 365

I have endured. I have accomplished the impossible, through charters written of dystopian apocalypse, succeeded where many have failed, and I have endured. I am blessed to be present, and I will continue to pursue the execution of my gift.

RAIN

I sometimes get lost in the clouds

and forget to plant my toes in the ground

my spirit takes flight

and soon I forget

That this isn't my first time around.

Everything feels new to me

and I love the light I touch

I mend it, pour it into love

and rain compassion,

filling every cup.

SWEETIE

Sweet tea, stuck to the roof of my mouth, formed like stalactites.

Alchemized from the poison I spit,

I sling healing words and disease my skin with talk of grisly distortion.

My right eye a glowing rose lens and my left blessed with the sight of abhorrent distinction.

I see the good in everyone, everything.

Everything but me.

So, I swallow my spit and hold my tongue in hopes that if it doesn't kill me first,

It'll cure me.

4.

CHARACTER

And that's where we differ.

You think your hopes and assumptions that a person could be good are a better testimony of their character than what they've shown you.

Have a little faith in people, they're often precisely who they tell you they would be.

5.

THE SUN

In my bones,

inspired by acrimonious love;

My body houses the sun.

With all its anger, it sparks a savage glow.

Courage cornered,

I've fathomed fear.

I understand now,

I'll take your hand now.

It gnaws at my needs,

knowing no one ever knocks.

Eradicating empathy,

mellowed a mighty heart.

I was made mortal.

Buried my burdens,

beneath a broken heart.

What pumps my blood isn't an organ,

but the feeling closest to me.

The star that knew me,

and kept me as his son.

6.

LOVELY OLD CRONE

Scarred by frost, I've lost my life to the cold.

Chained, I won't open my eyes to the truth.

My skin bleeds against the loving touch of iron old.

I imagine drapes of lavish gold

adorning a centerpiece of my immemorial youth.

A lively boy, in his self-righteousness never to be consoled.

You must age they said, and he did grow.

But he abandoned what he knew.

Who he was, he'll never be. That star's lost its glow.

Empty your veins, and sharpen those bones.

You've got a fight to lose.

Death becomes you, dead star. For this life, you'll never atone.

A dead light is of no use. You'll reap what they have sown.

Pain and cold will nourish that seed, when he's finally come to.

But the dark will nurture the dead, that lovely old crone.

7.

NOT ALONE

I am centuries of resistance. I am centuries of love, centuries of rage, centuries of battle. I am dirty laundry washed, dried, and stained still.

I am the birth of capitalism. I am the stench of decay hidden beneath false profits and faulty idols. The pains of burden, of victory. I am the skeleton in your closet, the skeleton key.

I am the initiative and the follow-through. I am the vessel and the spirit. I am the result of my people jaded by life in death because death seems to consume life now, not end it.

I am life. I am choices made and in the making. I am battles fought and battles prevented. I am lives given, taken, planted, and bestowed. I am not alone.

8.

STARDUST

Tired eyes.

Baked vanilla, cinnamon.

Lined with the soft scent of a child pulling the tree by his hand,

Walking the concrete tread.

I wonder what sunsets smell like

racing fairies down the path,

beating streetlights home.

The buzz of wings, hung by their neck. They glow every night at this hour.

My dreams died here.

My knees and the cement would scuffle.

They would bruise, but the concrete cracked.

So, a draw as I drew the end of the rainbow in front of my doorstep.

And my neighbor washed it away.

Because this was no place for that.

No place for joy, or for fairies dancing the stardust off their wings, or for trees who guide children home.

They were each cut down, mutilated, repurposed for the use of adults too soon cut off from love and nature. Ase.

I still try to smell the sunset, searching for stardust and hands offered. I'm still searching for the end of my rainbow.

9.

FEELING

How quickly it fills you, if you let it.

No matter what form it comes in,

or how the matter forms.

The essence or the virtue of life.

I wonder if you truly knew the magic you behold,

that feeling,

that thing that courses through your veins

weighs on your shoulders

Or shudders in your stomach.

The magic of feeling.

10.

GROWTH

When pain and betrayal carve a home out of you, they seem
to evolve.

Hurt loses its edge and even treachery turns its back on you.

Apathy swallows every brick, the knobs no longer turn and
broken lights no longer flicker.

With jaded walls, every square foot devours sound entirely.

Screams lose their wrath, and the tears no longer rise.

Love doesn't mean much anymore.

Not to anybody.

Not to you.

11.

STILL

A once glorious pond, muddled with doubt and critique turned inward.

All the life you host, all the beauty you nourish

You can't seem to want to be yourself.

Paradigm of a perverse perspective of perfection.

You'll never touch the roses the trees whisper about,

and still, you neglect your lilies.

Still,

You want to grow beyond your depth.

Your waters seep into the sediment, drained.

Spread so far, so thin.

You fight in vain, to garland your moss.

And all you should've asked of your heart was to still.

12.

DESERVING

I am the consequence of love.

The evocation of sublime submission

To your heart, in profound belief that I am deserving and worthy of the same love I share.

Love, I am a product of and love that starts with me.

13.

IS

I realize with sleep still in my eye

And the sun on the horizon.

That you won't love every second you're awake

But you'll live it.

You won't spend every moment reaching into thrill or curiosity,

or nourishing love and community.

Life isn't a mission, a journey, an adventure, or an obligation.

It isn't earned or awarded, it simply is.

And it is to be lived, simply.

14.

MOONLIGHT

Could you tell the Sun from the Moon,

if you weren't so scared of the night?

Could you offer your love in the embrace

of her celestial light?

Walk the dusk and see

the stars, the earth, the harmony.

The loving pull of the tide,

the sweet cradle of shade.

The Moon and her home,

this nurturing abode,

will never turn you away.

EDEN

I'd never built walls. I have planted flowers, fruit, and trees. I'd plowed dry and arid soil, poisoned with self hatred and criticism. I weeded out the anti-blackness, drained the homophobia from the land. I irrigated my beautiful garden, with consummate love and compassion. I turned every seed of disgust into branches of beauty, all blossoming with lively splendor, shining the antiquity and allure of my soul.

And although it took years,

because it took years,

I will guard Eden with life and limb.

Even if I am the only one to ever relish his fruit.

16.

COLOR

If everything had a color, I would paint hate white.

Alabaster cruelty, and shades of vulnerability.

Love would be black and all consuming. And life would be vibrant in its variety of brown, tan, green, and nebulous waves of blue. Simply, because it's so easy to lose your way and get swallowed up by all you believe life is meant to be. Think of how bright those lines of cerulean would look if only you lived life as it is.

Joy would be transparent, the way it should be. Free of any pollution or taint. I would use each color to stain my canvas, each hue fully utilized to fashion a world of luminous brilliance, a world where love and respect took residence in each brush.

17.

NEITHER

I am neither anchor nor arrow.

I will hold no friend at bay, and pierce no silence with a hand held out.

If my boat is the only ship in the harbor, so be it.

We will sail the seas searching for serendipity and my crew-mates will be love, joy, and appreciation.

I will yield my bow to no friend, aim my love at no familiar face.

I will instead turn the salient point inward,

and fire upon myself, into every crevice and crack

The affirmations, affections, and avowals I had so easily afforded my clansmen.

I will rain into myself all the love I'd dug up and poured into others. The love I uprooted will branch again into me, deservingly.

18.

I AM

I am love, for if I were anything else, I would simply cease to be.

And that would be an insufferable plague on the world,

for me to be anything but love.

19.

COLD

How does the cold feel

when your heart cannot feel love

Does it feel at ease?

Or does it succumb,

succumb to a warm facade?

To a lovely front?

Has it made a home?

A home in the winter frost

endemic love lost

Aboriginal

Love less the loveless

And love yourself more

Tepid bitter heart

You will beat again, my love.

If only for me.

23

20.

GOD

If I am of God and every piece of me is of her entirely,

Does it not serve to reason that I am him?

Is it not the obvious conclusion that all the validation I will ever need, will come from within?

All my wants and desires, the power to create and to alter, I've always had?

And that life isn't about finding me, it is not about piecing together that which already was, is, and will be.

But, learning to assess him.

Learning that love, admiration, even Godliness is not sourced externally.

It is built upon and exaggerated, with every moment I choose to look myself in the eye.

And every time I choose to love who I see, who I feel, who I am, and who I want to be.

IF I AM

Does the wind envy the earth,

does it loathe freedom?

I imagine the wind does not wish for stagnation,

Nor does a flame envy the pond's fluidity.

The ocean, in all its massiveness, does not aim to mimic the spark of an ember

The ground does not tremble searching for release.

We admonish that which we possess, for we do not love that which we are.

We do not love who we are.

But, I have learned

That if I am to be a river, I will rage in the torrent of every emotion.

If I am to be a gale, I will grace each blade of grass with my presence.

If I am of the earth, I will serve as great a foundation and nurturer than ever there was.

If I am to embody the flame, I will march on passionately and leave awe and inspiration in my wake.

Whatever I am to be, whoever I am to be,

I will do so and become them with all that I am

So not to lose any part of me to that that is without me.

WANTED

I once thought that the love I wanted, was the love I would receive

I used to think that I wanted to be wanted,

Simplified myself to be the object of your affection

Flattened all my layers, rounded all my edges

Just to make it easier to love me

And as I got smaller, lighter, easier to pick up and to discard

Sanded so much of me

Shaved so much of me away

Only as I got closer to the core of who I was did I realize

I was not pursuing your love, but searching for my own

I should not have been grinding my jagged edges against insecurity,

Scraping my sides with your validation.

I should have instead extended my reach

Sharpened my tips,

Added to my layers.

And gifted me the greatest blessing of

Unconditional self-love

Regardless of who else was there to experience it.

And now I realize that the love I wanted, is instead the love I would give

To myself.

BEAUTY

I want to be everything that is good in the world,

I want to be and embody love.

I want to be and embody peace.

I want to be and embody joy.

I will consume and become all the things that make this world beautiful.

And in return,

Become beautiful myself.

STANDING

Life, like anything else, should be taken standing up.

On your own two feet, or whatever you can manage really

to honor yourself,

the experience and everyone you come across

you should value every circumstance and choose to grow

standing through storm and serenity

through scarcity and sacrifice,

through sadness and satisfaction,

rooted securely in love and trust,

branch into every opportunity

finding light in every window

standing strong, Stoic

standing beautifully, bold

But standing still.

Through it all,

standing.

OLD FRIENDS

How do you look so familiar,

when we've been at odds this long?

Why do I find comfort in your embrace

Knowing loving you is wrong?

On the verge of disaster,

you've been the sole harbinger of peace

and I could master love forever

If only I'd remember me.

26.

ADEM OF(R)

Success is not something to be attained, but an expression.

For me, success is not a goal but a quality.

I am successful, and I could not indulge the absence of said trait.

With the centuries of sacrifice, thousands of heads bowed

Jewels stolen, ships downed.

I could not be anything but,

for it was not in my making.

I am successful because it lies in every detail, every day and every day past.

It is in each fiber, every cell.

I will be successful because in every person who awaited my arrival

They saw nothing but.

27.

HOME

I stepped into myself
and found my body suddenly afloat

in clouds of condensed dreams waiting to pour out from my
fingers

And rain all that I am into the world.

I could taste the silver dew in the air,

every atom shot soft fire into my nerves,

suddenly I knew where everything had its place.

I found peace for myself and in myself.

I found myself nowhere and everywhere all at once,

I found myself at home.

OBSIDIAN

My body is not a carriage, it is an anchor.

It refines my understanding,

like a gem rolled on sanded whetstone and grains of life.

An obsidian weight, dressed beautifully in black.

An onyx tether extended from my spirit into this physical realm, allowing me to assimilate all the gifts this life has to offer

Into the deepest part of me.

And to be allowed to take so much goodness

to bathe in such divinity,

while giving so little of my infinite time in return.

It is the greatest blessing indeed.

MAGIC

The only magic I wish to possess,

is the ability so remarkable that it remains the object of adulation since time long before.

To freeze time, the skill to capture every immaculate detail

without the loss of a rugged leaf hugging the wind,

or a single blade of grass afraid to let go of the earth.

I do not wish to become God,

but to empower him.

To transplant every moment of motivation,

every instant of innovation

And to share it with those who believe life to be without.

Simply to share all my wonders and simple joys, giving every one of you the opportunity to experience life's most unsung gifts.

And create the greatest symphony to ever pirouette these lush lands of green.

LOVING

There should be no pain in loving.

No fault in choosing to offer your adoration,

so love freely and willingly.

Without remorse or reservation,

watch how easily the world accommodates your divine
contribution.

www.ingramcontent.com/pod-product-compliance
Lightning Source LLC
LaVergne TN
LVHW010833200726

843508LV00012B/2580